LIBRARIES

Zartan

A Play

N. J. Warburton

Samuel French – London
New York – Sydney – Toronto – Hollywood

ISBN 0 573 12304 7

ZARTAN

First performed by SUDS (Stapleford Umbrella Drama Society) on 3rd April, 1987, with the following cast of characters:

Lord Greycoat	Peter Green
Gervaise	John Luckham
Waiter/Dr Wadding	Tim Ellis
Air Hostess	Lynn Pepperell
Gerald	Nick Warburton
Daphne	Carol Tomson
Armpits	Carol Green
Jane	Jackie Green
Zartan	Chris Evans

Produced by Kay Coe

AUTHOR'S NOTE

The action of the play is defined by the storytelling of Lord Greycoat. It should therefore be as uninterrupted as possible, each scene flowing into the next, the settings flexible and suggested, rather than solid and difficult to trundle on and off. The stewardess and Jane could be doubled. Gerald and Zartan could also be doubled. The apes are best represented by false ears, make-up and so on, rather than by full mask.

N. J. Warburton

ZARTAN

Lord Greycoat's Club

Greycoat and Gervaise are in the middle of a yarn-spinning session. They are crusty old characters. Gervaise has a habit of drifting off. An unctious Waiter glides in the background

Gervaise ... Turned out to be two sets of twins. Each with a wooden leg.
Greycoat Good Lord, you don't say so.
Gervaise Absolutely true. (*To the Waiter*) A couple more brandies for Lord Greycoat and myself, waiter.
Waiter (*gliding off*) Of course, sir.
Greycoat Just a minute, waiter.

Without stopping the Waiter glides back in a smooth arc

You're new here, aren't you?
Waiter Indeed I am, my lord.
Greycoat Thought I knew you, that's all.
Waiter Most unlikely, my lord. I move in much humbler circles. May I continue, my lord?
Greycoat Yes. Get on with it.

The Waiter glides off

Gervaise Creepy beggar, don't you think?
Greycoat Oily, I'd say Gervaise. As it should be with waiters.
Gervaise Indeed. Come on then, Greycoat. Your turn for a yarn.
Greycoat So it is. Did I ever tell you about the hard-boiled egg that cost me twenty-five thousand pounds and a night strapped to the Eiffel Tower?
Gervaise More than once.
Greycoat Oh. What about the Archbishop's harem in the wilds of Dartmoor?
Gervaise Yes. And the tale of the bare-knuckle brawl with the President of the Mineworkers' Union at the bottom of Gowthorp Shaft.

Greycoat Ah. Well . . . well . . .
Gervaise (*with relish*) That's it, Greycoat. You've run out of yarns, haven't you? Fifteen years we've been telling stories in this club and you've finally run out of things to say.

During the following, the Waiter enters unnoticed by Greycoat and Gervaise. He carries a tray with two glasses

Greycoat The time I crossed the Irish Sea in a suitcase to save a lady's honour?
Gervaise Yes!
Greycoat Damn. What about——
Gervaise What?
Greycoat —the day I lost my son?
Gervaise Good grief! Lost your son? Didn't know you had a son.
Greycoat You wouldn't. I lost him, you see.
Waiter Your drinks, gentlemen.
Gervaise } (*together; jumping*) { Good Lord!
Greycoat } { Good grief!
Gervaise Last chappie used to bump into tables. Knew he was coming.
Waiter Beg pardon, gentlemen. Stealth is something of a habit with me, acquired during my spell with Intelligence.

The Waiter exits

Gervaise Then, if I were you, I'd cultivate something of a new habit . . . (*He realizes the Waiter is not there*) Oh, he's gone. Did you hear that, Greycoat? Chappie had a spell with Intelligence.
Greycoat Sounds fishy to me. Fellow doesn't quite add up. You'd think they'd be able to spell in Intelligence without help from the likes of him.
Gervaise Never mind. You were telling me about this son of yours.
Greycoat So I was. It's something I've hardly told anyone in over twenty years. I found it all too . . . painful. I blame myself, you see. It all started on the day I took a cheap flight, tourist class, down to the Cape.
Gervaise Tourist class? Good grief. I'm sorry, Greycoat, it's never occurred to me that abject poverty was part of the colourful tapestry that makes up your life.

During the following, the airliner scene is set. A small case and a carry-cot are placed by the seat Greycoat is going to occupy. Other passengers may be sleeping in their seats

Greycoat Well, twenty years ago I had the estate to run and there were no wildlife parks in those days, you know. Had to save money, cut corners. Mind you, I should've been suspicious when I saw the crate they expected us to fly in . . .

He stands, walks into the airliner scene and sits down while Gervaise watches

Spluttering engine noises are heard and the passengers judder from time to time

(*Still narrating*) I had my son with me. He was only little and hidden in a sort of carry thing because I could scarce afford a ticket for him. It was a bumpy ride but eventually I managed to drop off.

Gervaise I say!

Greycoat To sleep, I mean. (*He sleeps*)

The engine splutters, the passengers judder

A Stewardess appears and makes her way up the aisle. She seems calm but she is actually neurotic from the flying hours she has spent living on her nerves

Stewardess There is nothing to worry about. Absolutely nothing. Everything is under control. The pilot knows exactly what he is doing.

She wakes Greycoat

Excuse me, my lord. Lord Greycoat.

Greycoat Hmm. What? What is it?

Stewardess Everything is under complete control, my lord. There's nothing to worry about.

Greycoat I wasn't worrying; I was asleep.

Stewardess I'm very pleased to hear it, my lord. Coolness in danger—I mean in flight. A true British characteristic. (*Indicating the other passengers*) Something the craven riffraff back there might take as an example.

The engine splutters

Greycoat There's nothing up, is there?
Stewardess (*laughing*) Good heavens, my lord, of course not. Apart from the plane, that is.
Greycoat The plane?
Stewardess Up in the air, my lord.

She laughs a ringing, false laugh, stopped by the engine cutting out for a moment

Greycoat Just a minute. There *is* something wrong!
Stewardess My word, hasn't it got warm all of a sudden? I expect we're over the jungle. I expect that's what it is. Do you mind if I remove my blouse? (*She starts to take her blouse off*)
Greycoat Listen, young lady. I've paid good money to be flown across Africa. I suspect that something is seriously wrong and that you are making a pathetic attempt to divert my attention. Well, let me tell you ... (*He notices that the blouse is now off*) I will not be fobbed off by ... by a couple of ...
Stewardess But I feel so much better, my lord. Aren't you feeling a little warm yourself?
Greycoat It won't work you know!

She is fiddling with his tie when the engine stops completely

What's that?
Stewardess What? I can't hear anything.
Greycoat Exactly. We should be hearing the engine.
Stewardess I expect they've switched the silencers on.

The Pilot is heard making inexpert engine noises, off

There we are, my lord. Nothing to worry about.
Greycoat That's not the engine. It's a man. It's the pilot!
Stewardess Is it?
Greycoat Of course it is. Listen.
Stewardess Oh yes. He must've come to again.
Greycoat Come to? What's going on here?
Stewardess Just turbulence, my lord. Won't last long.
Greycoat Why is the pilot making engine noises?
Stewardess Is this your hand luggage, my lord? Only it shouldn't really be here. I'll move it for you. (*She flings his case off*)
Greycoat (*leaping up*) I say!

Stewardess (*forcing him down*) Careful, my lord. You could find yourself sucked out.
Greycoat But you've just thrown my case off the plane!
Stewardess Standard landing procedure. Nothing to worry about.
Greycoat But I needed that.
Stewardess We have fully-trained operatives on the ground.
Greycoat But it contained . . .

The Stewardess picks up the carry-cot

Wait! DON'T TOUCH THAT!
Stewardess All ballast—I mean baggage—must be treated——
Greycoat But it's not baggage——

The Stewardess throws the carry-cot out

—it's a carry-cot!!
Stewardess A what?
Greycoat A carry-cot. I had a child in that!
Stewardess But you're a man, my lord.
Greycoat I mean I *kept* a child in it: my son.

The Pilot stops making engine noises, off

Listen! The pilot's cut out!
Stewardess Perfectly normal, believe me. Refuelling. Probably stopped for a drink.

Another false laugh and she dashes off

Greycoat continues his story as the plane is removed and bits of jungle are brought on

Greycoat We landed perfectly safely in the end. Apparently that sort of caper went on with every flight: keep the passengers happy and chuck something out if the thing got too wobbly. Still, there I was at the Cape without my case. Or my son. I kicked up a stink, of course, but it cut no ice. Round and round in bureaucratic circles, like trying to phone the Gas Board. However, deep inside me, I felt that young Theo had survived the drop.
Gervaise Theo, eh? Strange name for a case.
Greycoat No, Theo was the baby. I can't remember what I called

the case. Anyway, as I was to discover later, the baby did indeed plummet through the trees and come safely to rest . . .

They turn to watch as . . .

Gerald, Daphne and Armpits enter. They are apes, but rather middle-class and dressed for a country picnic

After a while the carry-cot flies in and lands near them

Armpits I say! Did you see that?
Daphne Stay where you are, Armpits. You don't know where it's been.
Gerald Yes. Quite. Er . . . What do you suggest we do about this, Daphne?
Daphne Nothing at all. Leave it where it is. It's nothing to do with us.
Gerald I don't know, dear. It looks like quality baggage to me.
Armpits We can't just leave it, Mummy. It's snuffling.
Daphne It's a ploy, dear. Trying to attract attention to itself.
Gerald Perhaps we ought to take a peep. Just to see.
Armpits Oh yes, Daddy! Do let's! Please!
Daphne Armpits! Control yourself! It's not a toy we're talking about. Are you serious, Gerald? Take a look? Have you any idea what that might lead to?
Gerald It can't do any harm.
Daphne Oh, can't it? What about those apes who lived the other side of the swamp? The Palmers? What about them?
Gerald What about them?
Gerald They found a baby in a case, just like this one, crashed through the trees. And what happened? Before they knew what was what they were bringing it up as one of their own. You know I hate racial prejudice, Gerald, but that is disgusting. Apart from the fact that it was another mouth to feed they had absolutely no idea about its background. And it was so puny. No grip to speak of, and I hate that in a child.

The sound of marching feet is faded up and Armpits goes to investigate this

Armpits I say, Daddy. Ants!
Gerald Not now, Armpits. I'm listening to your mother.

Armpits moves around the stage following an invisible trail of ants

Gerald Then there was Mr and Mrs Priestley, that chimpanzee couple. They found a baby in a duty-free carrier bag and they took it in because they thought it would be company for the boys . . .

Gerald Well in a way . . .

Gerald Have you forgotten the endless problems they had to endure after that?

Gerald It wasn't all that bad . . .

Gerald All those humans tramping the place flat looking for the baby. With their ridiculous little sandwiches and their foul-smelling socks draped over the bushes to dry . . .

Gerald And their film contracts.

Daphne And those laughable shorts, and . . . what?

Armpits Mummy, I think the ants have seen the baby too.

Daphne Your father and I are talking business, Armpits. Don't interrupt. Go on, Gerald.

Gerald Well, I don't fancy some hairless infant puking all over the jungle any more than you do but you must admit that both the Palmers and the Priestleys did rather well out of it in the end. Mrs Palmer had that small part in *Life on Earth* with David Attenborough; and the Priestleys were signed up for those tea commercials . . .

The carry-cot slowly slides off the stage, noticed only by Armpits. The sound of marching feet fades down

Daphne That's right. And Mrs Palmer wasn't really that good. So stiff and simpering all the time.

Gerald You said yourself you'd've made a better job of it. I mean, with your body . . .

Armpits Mummy, Daddy, the baby's gone.

Gerald } (*together*) { Oh.
Daphne } { What?

Daphne Gerald! Look at that! It's being carried off by common ants. Stop them, for goodness' sake!

Gerald (*without moving*) I say! You chaps!

Daphne Gerald!

Gerald dashes off after the carry-cot but returns almost at once

Gerald It's no good, dear. There's no stopping that lot when they get going.
Armpits (*whimpering*) Oh Daddy! The poor little thing.
Daphne (*to Gerald*) I blame you for this.
Gerald Now what?
Daphne You're so indecisive, Gerald. If only you'd made a snap decision when the baby first appeared.
Gerald But I——
Daphne But oh no! We have to dither. It might be weeks before we get another chance like this. Oh, stop whining, Armpits!

She clips Armpits and storms off

Armpits wails

Gerald Shut up, Armpits!

He also clips Armpits and they both trail off

As Greycoat continues his story, the jungle pieces are replaced by a screen behind which Jane takes up position

Greycoat The years went by and I knew nothing of all this. But there remained this nagging belief that Theo was still alive . . .
Gervaise Which he was. Brought up by apes.
Greycoat No! By ants. The apes were too slow; somewhat like you, Gervaise, if I may say so. I do wish you'd keep up. Anyway, I did all that flesh and blood could to trace my son: absolutely pestered Lost Luggage with postcards; but nothing came of it. Then I came home and began to keep a few wild animals on my estate. This proved very popular and, at last, things began to take off.
Gervaise Oh bad luck. Just when you were getting yourself sorted out.
Greycoat What?
Gervaise Flew away, did they?
Greycoat No, I mean the *estate* took off; commercially. I was able to employ a first rate assistant and once again my thoughts began to turn to Africa. (*He crosses to the screen as jungle noises begin to sound. He listens for a while, looking grim*) All right, Jane. You can take it off now.
Jane (*behind the screen*) Yes, Lord Greycoat.
Greycoat (*glancing behind the screen*) I meant the record, Jane.

Jane (*behind the screen*) Oh. Sorry.

The jungle noises stop abruptly and Jane emerges

Why do you torture yourself like this, Lord Greycoat? Listening to the same old record of jungle noises over and over again.

Greycoat I . . . I have to, Jane.

Jane You can borrow my swinging chart-toppers.

Greycoat No, no. I have to listen to that record, Jane. For the sake of my son.

Jane Your son makes records? I didn't know that. I didn't even know you had a son.

Greycoat A lot of people don't know that. But the fact is, many years ago I was flying across Africa when a stewardess threw my son out of the plane.

Jane Oh, that is terrible!

Greycoat I have suffered.

Jane That's really awful. I mean, I'm not all that keen on the record myself but . . .

Greycoat It wasn't because of the record, Jane

Jane You mean, she liked it?

Greycoat No.

Jane Then what was he doing?

Greycoat He wasn't doing anything. She just threw him out. He was a baby at the time.

Jane Didn't she like babies?

Greycoat She didn't say. Anyway, that's why I listen to the record. It helps to keep hope fresh inside me.

Jane It must've been a bitter blow to lose such a talented child.

Greycoat Talented? He was only a baby.

Jane Exactly. All those animal impressions. It's fantastic in one of such tender years.

Greycoat He didn't make the record, Jane. I'm trying to tell you. I listen to the record because it reminds me of the jungle and the jungle reminds me of my son.

Jane Oh I see. (*Pause*) Someone else made the record?

Greycoat What? I don't know. I have no idea who made the record. That's not the point. I believe my son is still alive. I'm going back for him, Jane. That's why I asked to see you.

Jane Me?

Greycoat Yes. I need someone with your keen intelligence to help me organize an expedition to Africa. Use what funds I have from the wildlife park. Spare no expense. The time has come to act!

Jane Yes, my lord.

Jane exits

The screen is removed and bits of jungle returned as Greycoat continues his story

Greycoat So we got our expedition together. Friends said I was a fool but they'd been saying that for years so it didn't stop me. I was driven by hope, the fond hope that some kindly creature had rescued and nurtured Theo and that he'd grown up to be some kind of Lord of the Jungle.

Gervaise Seems reasonable.

Greycoat Well, you'd think so, wouldn't you? But things didn't work out quite as I imagined. Theo had survived but he wasn't feeling like a lord of the jungle.

They turn to watch as ...

Zartan (Theo) enters and sits dejectedly. Armpits, now grown up, also enters

Armpits Ah, Zartan. I've been looking for you everywhere.

Zartan Oh hello, Armpits.

Armpits There's something strange going on. Odd-looking creatures have been spotted in the jungle.

Zartan Really? They can't be much odder looking than me.

Armpits Oh no. Not morbid self-analysis again.

Zartan I'm sorry, Armpits, but it's no use pretending. I have to face up to the failure that I am.

Armpits But you've been facing up to that for years. You're always going on about what a flop you are. You're remarkably eloquent about it.

Zartan Do you really think so?

Armpits It's one of the few things you're good at.

Zartan You're just saying that to cheer me up, and it's no good. I'm a failure, a misfit. As an ant I'm a complete wash-out.

Armpits As an ant maybe ...

Zartan (*sudden despair*) I have so little in common with the other ants, Armpits. I don't even look like them.

Armpits Now don't upset yourself. Of course you do.
Zartan I don't. I'm bigger than they are for a start.
Armpits Are you? I can't say I'd noticed.
Zartan It's sweet of you to say so but you know I'm bigger than the other ants.
Armpits Well . . . a shade, perhaps.
Zartan A shade? Thousands of times bigger. I'm gross.
Armpits All right, all right, you're bigger . . . Considerably bigger. But does it matter, Zartan? Does it really matter? Is it something to get so depressed about?
Zartan Yes, Armpits, I'm afraid it is. People do get depressed about excess weight, you know. It's perfectly natural: unlike the rest of me. In my condition I'd've thought I was entitled to feel a touch glum. To say nothing of the legs.
Armpits What's wrong with your legs?
Zartan (*hysterical*) For pity's sake, Armpits! There are only four! I'm a pair short! It's so embarrassing, especially when I'm on guard duty at the hill. The number of times I've had to bluff my way through drill on account of those missing limbs.
Armpits Yes, but look on the bright side. OK, you're big but doesn't that make you a formidable opponent?
Zartan Formidable? Ha! Don't make me laugh. (*He bends over*) All right, Armpits, take a look at that and tell me what you see.
Armpits (*embarrassed*) Don't do that, Zartan. Sit down and compose yourself.
Zartan Just tell me what it is. It's a bum, isn't it? My bum. Yes?
Armpits Yes, well . . . ?
Zartan And what, pray, do you notice about it?
Armpits Look, I don't know what you're getting at here.
Zartan Just tell me what you see.
Armpits Well, it's pink . . .
Zartan I feel so ashamed!
Armpits Yes, all right. It's pink and the others aren't. Sit down. Point taken.
Zartan But that's just it. It has no point. It's completely pointless!
Armpits Of course it's got a point. You couldn't sit down without it.
Zartan I mean it has no point, no pointy bit, no sting. It's just there: round and blunt and pink. It disgusts me!
Armpits Pull yourself together; you're getting hysterical. You

can't go through life hating your own bum, Zartan. It isn't healthy.

Zartan I can't help hating it. It makes me feel so ... so inadequate.

Armpits Well, I wonder ... I wonder if you've ever considered ...

Zartan What?

Armpits Perhaps you're not a true ant.

Zartan Don't be ridiculous, Armpits. What else could I be?

Armpits Well I've been meaning to have a chat about this ...

Jane (*off*) This way, your lordship. Follow me.

Armpits No time now, Zartan. Those creatures I told you about. They're coming. Quick, hide!

They dash behind a bit of jungle

Greycoat Of course, I knew nothing of my son's identity crisis at the time. I had problems of my own. My main concern was with my outfit.

Gervaise Tricky. What does one wear in the jungle if one wishes to keep up appearances?

Greycoat I mean my team, my crew. Of course the bearers had all fled. They always do. Wouldn't set foot in the mystic realm of what they called the "Weird White Monster" unless they got time and a half. That left me and Jane and a sort of dogsbody by the name of Wadding. Strange chappie. Couldn't quite make him out.

Jane enters, carrying a handbag and a pith-helmet

She hands Greycoat the pith-helmet. There are jungle noises as he crosses to join her

(*To Jane*) Strangely impressive, isn't it, my dear?

Gervaise Yes indeed.

Greycoat I was talking to Jane. We're in flashback now, Gervaise. You really have the most annoying habit of dropping off.

Gervaise Sorry.

Greycoat Strangely impressive, isn't it, my dear?

Jane Yes, and sort of comforting too.

Greycoat Comforting?

Jane Yes. It reminds me of home, sitting in your study, listening to your son's record ...

Greycoat It wasn't my son's record. Listen, Jane. I have something on my mind. I'm worried about Wadding.
Jane I shouldn't worry, my lord. It's probably the heat.
Greycoat I mean Dr Wadding, our expedition colleague. I find him a bit creepy, Jane. He's always popping up when you least . . .

Wadding glides on behind them

Wadding Dinner is served!

Jane and Greycoat leap with shock

Wadding glides off

Jane Ah, Dr Wadding. Wonderful. Dinner is served, my lord.
Greycoat See what I mean? I don't like it, Jane. I don't like it. (*He starts to go out*)
Jane It's just his way, my lord. I'm sure he means nothing by it.

Greycoat exits

(*Calling*) Wadding!

Wadding suddenly appears again

Wadding What?
Jane Come over here! Just watch yourself. I've warned you about your suspicious behaviour.
Wadding I haven't done anything.
Jane No? Then what's that sticking out of your tent?
Wadding What? Nothing.
Jane Don't try it on with me, Wadding. You've been stuffing things again, haven't you?
Wadding The evenings are long in these parts, Miss, and a man's got to have a hobby.
Jane It's not a hobby. It's an unsavoury perversion. To think I hired an obsessive taxidermist for an expedition to a jungle! Why didn't you mention this at the interview?
Wadding You didn't ask.
Jane What is that thing in your tent?
Wadding It's just a trifle.
Jane Wadding!
Wadding It's a lion. I'm afraid I had to abandon it while I got the dinner ready.

Jane How repulsive! This has got to stop, Wadding. I hired you because you said you could handle animals.
Wadding And so I can.
Jane I didn't mean like that! Now get over to your tent and cover up that half-stuffed lion.
Wadding All right, I'm going; but you'll regret speaking to me in that high and mighty tone.

Wadding exits

Jane stoops to rummage in her bag

Zartan and Armpits come out again

Armpits What do you make of all this, Zartan?
Zartan It's incredible. Other ants, my size.
Armpits I'm not so sure they're ants . . .
Zartan Of course they are. I'm going to speak to this one.
Armpits Wait, Zartan. It might be dangerous.
Zartan (*to Jane*) Hello there.

Jane sees him and screams

Armpits, frightened, rushes off

Zartan is also shocked, but his mood is changed: he is now exuberant

Gosh, I'm sorry. I didn't mean to startle you.
Jane Oh. My word. That's all right. I thought you were Dr Wadding.
Zartan No, no. You know this is really amazing. I was just getting depressed about being the only ant around here this size . . .
Jane Sorry? The only what?
Zartan Ant. And out of the blue here are three others also odd and overweight . . .
Jane Ant?
Zartan Yes. Of course, I don't wish to appear rude. I don't think you're odd . . .
Jane You think you're an ant?
Zartan Yes. I can't tell you what it means to meet other ants like me . . .
Jane And you think I'm an ant?
Zartan Yes. My name's Zartan, by the way. And you are?
Jane Me? Jane.

Zartan Lovely.

Pause. They look at each other

I must introduce you to Armpits
Jane No, really! I'd rather not.
Zartan It's all right. He's an ape but he's an OK ape. (*Running off*) Armpits! Armpits!

Zartan exits

Jane Armpits? Ants? What is all this?

Greycoat enters

Greycoat (*crossing to her*) Jane, my dear, we're ready to start and, to be frank, I'm not at all happy about being alone in the tent with Wadding. There's something about the way he looks at me.
Jane Lord Greycoat, I think we may be on to something.
Greycoat Really?
Jane I've just met a man who thinks he's an ant.
Greycoat What?
Jane An ant.
Greycoat An ant? How many legs did he have?
Jane That's just it. He was exactly like you and me.
Greycoat Four, you mean?
Jane Four?
Greycoat Two for you and two for me.
Jane No, no. Two.
Greycoat Two? Then he was deceiving you, my dear. That was no ant.
Jane But Lord Greycoat, you don't think he could possibly be—
Greycoat —someone pretending to be an ant. Indeed I do, Jane.
Jane No, no. I mean someone brought up as an ant.
Greycoat I shouldn't think so. Who'd want to bring up a child as an ant?
Jane An ant would.
Greycoat I'm sorry Jane. I'm not with this.
Jane Just imagine: somehow a baby appears here in the jungle, is found by ants and carried off to their hill where the queen, recognizing some aristocractic streak in him, takes a fancy to him. He learns the ways of an ant and knows nothing of his true origins.

Greycoat (*after some pondering*) By George, Jane. I think you're right! That could just explain it. Shall we go into dinner now?
Jane But Lord Greycoat! This could be your son!
Greycoat What?
Jane Your son. I've just seen him and he had your nose.
Greycoat (*clutching his face*) My nose?
Jane Yes. He looked like you!
Greycoat Then we must act fast. (*Calling*) Wadding!

Wadding glides on

Wadding Yes?
Greycoat Oh, there you are. Fetch a net. We're going to trap an ant.
Jane But there's no need for a net, my lord.
Wadding No. It'll get through the holes. You want a jam jar.
Greycoat Must you be so dense, Wadding? This is no ordinary ant: this is my son!
Wadding Of course.
Greycoat It must be. Fully-grown, four legs, thinks it's an ant with my nose. It's too much of a coincidence to be anything else.
Wadding You mean a giant ant? Human size?
Greycoat Certainly.
Wadding I've never stuffed an ant before.
Jane Wadding!
Wadding This could be a taxidermy first. Not just a stuffed ant but one related to a peer of the realm. (*With a look at Greycoat*) And the peer himself! Yes, why not?
Jane Wadding! I warned you . . .
Wadding Oh, why pretend anymore? I came out here to get at the animals. I was born to stuff, not to act as some old duffer's lackey!
Greycoat What is he talking about, Jane? I only asked him to fetch a net.

As Jane explains, Wadding begins to measure Greycoat up

Jane It would appear, my lord, that he wishes to stuff Theo, followed, I regret to surmise, by you and probably me.
Greycoat Stuff? You mean he's prepared too much dinner?
Jane No, my lord.
Wadding Why not? There's a market for it!

Greycoat You cad, Wadding!
Wadding (*whipping out a knife*) And I'll begin at once.
Jane Put that knife away, you fool. You'll never get away with this!
Wadding Of course I will. What is there to stop me?

Zartan appears behind Wadding. He stops in his tracks looking puzzled

Jane Not another step, Wadding. Zartan is right behind you!
Wadding You must take me for a complete fool.
Jane Quick, Zartan. Get him!
Zartan Who?

Wadding spins round at the sound of Zartan's voice and Jane knocks the knife from his hand. Wadding and Zartan then circle each other, preparing to fight

Jane Overpower him, Zartan! Quick!

Zartan suddenly whips round and offers to sting Wadding

Wadding, completely thrown, runs off with Zartan and Jane in pursuit

The jungle noises stop. Greycoat returns to Gervaise to continue the story

Greycoat So we had the narrowest of escapes and I was rescued by a son who, the last time I'd seen him, had been plummeting through the air in a carry-cot. Wadding, I'm sorry to say, managed to give us the slip and hasn't been seen since. We decided that Theo's return to the country of his birth should be delayed. The sight of him trying to sting the manic taxidermist was enough to convince me that he was not ready for any but the stranger backwaters of English public life. He remained in the jungle, and Jane remained with him, attempting, as she put it, to rehabilitate him. After much patient therapy, they felt they were ready to face civilization and so they took the next logical step.
Gervaise Logical Step, eh? Can't say I know them.
Greycoat What? Know who?
Gervaise Logical Step. Airline, are they?
Greycoat What are you talking about?
Gervaise Next Logical Step out of Africa . . .

Greycoat No. I mean they did the next thing that made the most sense. Which is more than you've ever done.
Gervaise So what did they do?
Greycoat They wrote a letter of resignation to the Queen Ant.

Jane and Zartan enter with a letter

Jane You're sure about this, Zartan?
Zartan Positive.
Jane And you no longer think you're an ant?
Zartan What? Me an ant? With only four legs?
Jane Two legs, Zartan. Two legs and two arms.
Zartan Oh yes. Of course.
Jane Right. (*Reading*) "Your Royal Highness . . ."
Zartan We can't say "highness". She's touchy about height.
Jane You ought to be more firm, Zartan. Put your foot down.
Zartan And you certainly can't put your foot down. Not in an ant hill. Here let me see. (*He takes the letter and reads*) "The time has come for me to leave and set up a hill——"
Jane A home.
Zartan "—a home of my own. I am grateful for all you and the lads have done for me. If ever your foraging should take you to London, Jane and I will always be pleased to see you. Best wishes. Zartan."
Jane Good. Brief and to the point.

Zartan sucks in his breath, wounded by this

Now then, Zartan. Keep a grip on yourself. Humans don't have points, right?
Zartan Right.
Jane Right. Now let's deliver this letter. How should we do that?
Zartan Leave it on one of the trails. It'll either get taken straight to Her Majesty or chewed to a pulp.
Jane You see? Not so very different from the way things are done at home. Come on.

Zartan and Jane exit

During the following, the Waiter furtively enters and takes position behind Gervaise's chair

Greycoat (*to Gervaise*) And then, only this morning in fact, this arrived. (*He takes out a small box and a tiny, stamp-sized piece of paper*) A letter from the Queen Ant. Just listen to this, Gervaise. (*Reading*) "Dear Lord Greycoat, it has been brought to our notice that Zartan is your son. We must confess that the news is something of a relief to us since we had fallen into the habit of thinking he was one of ours and this had caused us much pondering on our past movements. Still, when one has twenty-five thousand children at a time, one is inclined to get a little muddled. However, all is now well and we are happy to return him to you. The box is for Zartan and contains a surprise for him and Jane. Yours etc. Helen Regina." Isn't that marvellous? I wonder what's in the box. Well, no doubt we'll find out soon enough because Theo should be, at this very moment, on his way to the Club. (*Pause*) Gervaise? (*Silence*)

No answer

Good Lord, man, you haven't dropped off?

Slowly the Waiter emerges from behind Gervaise's chair, a manic smile on his face

I say, what are you doing there? Don't you know the meaning of a discreet distance?

Waiter But, my lord, I can't do what I have to do if I keep my distance, can I?

Greycoat I don't know. What do you have to do?

Waiter Come, come. Surely you know who I am?

Greycoat No.

The Waiter snatches off his bow-tie and is recognized at once

Wadding!!

Wadding Indeed, my lord. Back to complete a little unfinished business.

Greycoat And just as careless, I see. All right, Gervaise, get him!

No answer

Now, Gervaise. Pounce!

Wadding I wouldn't waste your breath, Lord Greycoat.

Greycoat Good grief, man, you haven't . . .

Wadding And neither of you noticed a thing! Sheer genius! A masterpiece!

Greycoat I can't believe this. I must be dreaming.
Wadding Not a dream, my lord. A nightmare, perhaps. And as for your friend, shall we just say his little sleep was rounded with a stuff.
Greycoat You cad!
Wadding We'll begin by opening that box, shall we?

Greycoat starts to open the box

Zartan and Jane enter

They are drawn to the box and peering in when Greycoat looks up and sees them

Greycoat Theo, my boy!

Wadding spins round

Zartan Clive?

Wadding spins back

Greycoat Jane!

Wadding spins round

Zartan Simon! What are you doing here?

Wadding spins back, now quite dizzy

Jane Wadding!

Wadding spins back and is about to totter

Zartan (*helping him*) Steady on, there, my friend.
Greycoat Oh Theo, you fool! You could've pounced! Now you've missed your chance.
Wadding (*pulling a gun*) Indeed he has. Keep still, all of you.
Jane Don't be angry with Zartan, Lord Greycoat. We came to seek a blessing on our union.
Greycoat Good God, Theo, you haven't joined a union? First my best friend is stuffed by a crazed taxidermist and now my son wants to join a union. It's more than an old man can bear.
Jane It's not that kind of union, Lord Greycoat.
Greycoat And who the devil are Clive and Simon? Five minutes in this country and the boy's gone right off his head.
Zartan Clive and Simon are friends, Father. From Africa.

Wadding Look, do you mind sorting this out later. Only, I'm the one with the gun.

Greycoat Just a minute, just a minute. You say Clive and Simon are friends?

Zartan Yes.

Jane And you've just called out their names?

Zartan That's right.

Greycoat Then why can't you get them to help us?

Wadding That's enough! I'm fed up with being ignored like this. I don't care who or what Clive and Simon are. They're too late! You're all under my power now! (*He laughs*)

Zartan We'll see about that! OK, Clive. OK, Simon. Get him!

Wadding, Greycoat and Jane look left, right and back. Nothing happens

Wadding They don't seem to be taking very much notice, Ant Man.

Zartan Oh yes they do.

Wadding Then where, pray, are they?

Zartan Well, they *were* in that box my father is holding.

Greycoat The box from Africa. Good heavens!

Jane And where are they now?

Zartan Half-way up the inside of Wadding's trouser legs!

Wadding Ants?!

Zartan Ants indeed, Wadding. Sent over by the Queen herself to attend our wedding in the Abbey. Now drop that gun or it'll be the worse for you!

Wadding Never!

Zartan Right, lads! Now!

Wadding raises his gun then screams and clutches himself. Zartan and Greycoat shake hands. Jane simpers. They all hold a tableau

Black-out

FURNITURE AND PROPERTY LIST

On stage: Table
Two armchairs

Off stage: Tray with two glasses **(Waiter)**
Plane seats **(Stage Management)**
Small case **(Stage Management)**
Carry-cot **(Stage Management)**
Bits of jungle **(Stage Management)**
Carry-cot **(Stage Management)**
Screen **(Stage Management)**
Pith-helmet **(Jane)**
Letter **(Jane)**

Personal: **Jane:** handbag
Wadding: knife, gun (in pocket)
Greycoat: small box, tiny piece of paper (in pocket)

LIGHTING PLOT

Simple interior and exterior settings

Practical fittings required: nil

To open:	Full general lighting	
Cue 1:	They all hold a tableau	(Page 21)
	Black-out	

EFFECTS PLOT

Cue 1	The airliner scene is set *When ready, spluttering engine noises*	(Page 3)
Cue 2	**Greycoat**: *"To sleep, I mean."* *Engine splutters*	(Page 3)
Cue 3	**Stewardess**: "... might take as an example." *Engine splutters*	(Page 3)
Cue 4	The **Stewardess** laughs a ringing, false laugh *Cut engine for a moment*	(Page 4)
Cue 5	The **Stewardess** fiddles with **Greycoat's** tie *Cut engine noises*	(Page 4)
Cue 6	**Stewardess**: "... switched the silencers on." *Fake engine noises, off*	(Page 4)
Cue 7	**Greycoat**: "... a child in it: my son." *Cut fake engine noises*	(Page 5)
Cue 8	**Daphne**: "... I hate that in a child." *Fade up sound of marching feet*	(Page 6)
Cue 9	The carry-cot slowly slides off *Fade down sound of marching feet*	(Page 7)
Cue 10	**Greycoat** crosses to the screen *Jungle noises*	(Page 8)
Cue 11	**Jane**: "Oh. Sorry." *Cut jungle noises*	(Page 9)
Cue 12	**Jane** hands **Greycoat** the pith-helmet *Jungle noises*	(Page 12)
Cue 13	**Wadding** runs off with **Zartan** and **Jane** in pursuit *Cut jungle noises*	(Page 17)

MADE AND PRINTED IN GREAT BRITAIN BY
LATIMER TREND & COMPANY LTD PLYMOUTH
MADE IN ENGLAND